tant

YOU ARE BEAUTIFUL

YOU ARE BEAUTIFUL

A GUIDE TO INNER PEACE

NADYA GIUSI

WITH ILLUSTRATIONS BY
ELDON DEDINI

CARMEL PRODUCTIONS
225 Crossroads Blvd., Suite 406
Carmel, CA 93923-8649
www.nadyagiusi.com

Cover and book design:
Bunne Hartmann, Hartmann Design Group

Illustrations: Eldon Dedini

ISBN 978-0-9623548-0-9

Library of Congress Cataloging-in-Publication Data

To Eric Berne, my friend,
who told me I was beautiful
which got me thinking
that maybe he knew
something about me
I didn't.

Also by the author

The New Family:
Mapping Your Way to the Good Stuff!

CONTENTS

Be a light unto yourself
Do not go after others
Do not follow others
Be your own lamp
This is my message.

– from Sayings of the Buddha

THE BACKSTORY

A Mystic Experience

If I say to you that you are beautiful
and you deny it
then what has happened is that your wall,
which you built as a child – in order to survive –
has become so strong
you are afraid to tear it down.

ABOUT THE BOOK

The book is divided into two sections: The Backstory and The Message. The Backstory tells you how the message came to be. The Message is the message itself accompanied by a process to help you learn the lessons it offers and adapt them to your everyday life. I have also included illustrations by Eldon Dedini, not only to amuse and delight you, but to help you anchor the message and reinforce what you are learning. There is also space for you to put down your own doodles, drawings and notes as you read along.

It Takes A Village is in place of acknowledgments at the back of the book. No one accomplishes a task, like the writing of a book and bringing it to market, alone. The names listed belong to real people. Real people who are my friends. Real people who have lives of their own but who have been willing to help me because they believe in me and in the project. It Takes A Village is their story, a story of their kindness, their friendship, and of their dedication to the strength and beauty of the human spirit.

HOW IT HAPPENED

I was sitting in my garden one afternoon testing the microphone of a tape recorder that I had just bought at Macy's. It was the first of its kind – small enough to fit into the palm of my hand – and, as I began to speak, there was no sense of effort or forethought. The words, "You are beautiful. You don't know that, do you? But you are. Beautiful," simply came out of my mouth. Twenty-eight minutes later the words stopped.

The next day I had an irresistible impulse to continue speaking. It was as if I had no choice. I went back to the same chair in my garden, turned the tape over and more words came through without interruption. Twenty-seven minutes later, the words stopped as abruptly as they had the day before. Both sides of the sixty-minute tape were full.

This story really begins, however, fourteen years earlier when Eric Berne, my dear friend and mentor, said to me, "Nadya, you are beautiful." By instinct I pulled back, as I did at any compliment, and I could feel my skin turning red all over my body. But, unconsciously, I must have stored his words away in a hidden corner of my mind – like a squirrel gathering nuts for winter – and I forgot about them.

Eric was my weekend beach pal. He was also the psychiatrist who became famous as the "father of transactional analysis." His book *Games People Play* was a phenomenal success, a *New York Times* bestseller which was translated into over a dozen foreign languages. His life changed as a result of his success but our relationship didn't. He continued driving down from San Francisco to Carmel on weekends, bringing with him freshly baked bagels to share. We still hung out with our children at the beach at Stewart's Point on Saturdays. And, on many Sunday evenings during crab season, we would buy a couple of cooked, cracked crabs and sit around our kitchen table with a loaf of sourdough bread, a tossed green salad, and gorge. When Johnny

Carson invited him on the Tonight Show, Eric came over with two neckties in hand saying, very seriously, "Nadya, which one should I wear?" After Eric died in 1970, I missed my old friend very much.

On that afternoon in my garden in 1982 when I heard the words, "You are beautiful," they were so insistent I couldn't ignore them – as I had when Eric had said them years before. Furthermore, since "The Message" (as I have come to call it) seemed to come from somewhere inside myself, there was no way I could fight it, explain it or deny it.

I was fifty. I had been married twenty-six years. I had just moved through a period of transition and loss that had dragged me out of a world I knew and understood into a world unknown. My two daughters had left for college and my mother had died. My career was threatened as well because I began to suffer from spinal scoliosis resulting from a fused hip due to a childhood bout with bone cancer. In the early sixties I had established three successful Montessori schools and a teacher-training center; these demanded a physical flexibility that I no longer possessed. A major portion of my identity had been tied up in my work with the children, but now, I faced losing their presence in my life and the powerful connection we had together. The grief I felt set me spinning. My life no longer seemed to have purpose or direction. Struggling, I turned toward spiritual matters, including the practice of Yoga. Eventually I gained enough distance from my pain to take a deep breath and think to myself, "Okay, what now?" In 1977 I went back to graduate school to become a marriage and family therapist with a specialty in clinical hypnosis.

ABOUT THE CD

After I received The Message, my assistant Elaine, who was as stunned as I was about the whole event, transcribed it. Again, a few weeks later, I had another irresistible urge to pass on what had been given to me although I wasn't sure how. Then, one afternoon I took a pair of scissors and began cutting up the paragraphs that Elaine had so carefully transcribed, laid them down in strips all over my living room floor and started sorting through them. Paying careful attention to the integrity of the text, I rearranged the words into a coherent story and added an introduction and an ending. The result became a guided meditation, a narration that I then recorded with music specially written for the project by the composer Malcolm Seagraves.

This audio cassette succeeded beyond anything I could have expected. Even though I took it off the market some years ago, it has gathered somewhat of a cult following. I still get requests for it. The original version, issued in 1982, has turned up at our community hospital in the psychiatric ward, a beauty salon in Los Angeles, and has been as popular with men as it has with women. People tell me they play and replay the tape "because I hear something new every time."

Now The Message has found new life in book form with Eldon Dedini's charming drawings, I am reissuing the guided meditation as a CD with the original narration but a different score. Interestingly, the present version was actually the first recording I did twenty years ago and decided not to use. Rediscovering it has been a happy accident because it sounds bright and modern in its new incarnation as an extension of the book.

When you listen you will notice that not every line precisely follows the text. You will also notice that the music does not hide behind the spoken word, as an accompaniment would do. The words and music are designed as one all embracing sound to help unify the mind, the body and the spirit through an experience of total immersion. For this reason I suggest that you not play the CD while driving. It will relax you and could make you drowsy. Instead, play it in part or in its entirety when you have the time to focus completely, to absorb it and to relax.

For the full experience, practice the Yoga Asana *Savasana* – also known as The Relaxation Pose – as you listen. On the first track I lead you, step-by-step, through this ancient mindfulness exercise. You can either use it to prepare yourself for hearing The Message or you may practice *Savasana* separately any time you simply want to spend a few moments in a completely relaxed state.

ABOUT REINCARNATION

There is a strong bias for the belief in reincarnation in The Message. As I have said, I did not compose the text. The text came to me as a complete whole, already composed. My own spiritual background has been solidly Christian – I was baptized and confirmed in the Episcopal Church. But because my mother was born and educated in Japan, as was her mother, and because I grew up in the Far East until I was nine years old, the teachings of the Buddha were very much a part of our household. Even so, I was surprised when the notion of reincarnation resurfaced over forty years later in the form of past lives while I was practicing clinical hypnosis in graduate school.

Regression work – taking a client back to repressed memories through hypnosis – is standard procedure in dealing with hidden resistance or trauma. However, while in a trance, some of my clients returned to the womb and other lifetimes to find answers to their pain. Not only did I find this material startling but I also found that the results of this work were often quite dramatic. To preserve a scientific approach, I did not discount these supernatural life stories. I documented them. So, I must confess, at the time I first heard The Message, I was already spending a lot of time rummaging around in the unconscious mind. Whether this fact projected itself on The Message as it was coming through me or whether the words are pure spirit, I cannot say. I only know that I felt like a vessel that was completely open. The fact is, this whole experience, which I am at a loss to explain, has become a profound mystical process that has changed my life.

ABOUT THE PROCESS

Many of us carry on a futile dialogue in our heads, which sounds more like a debate between two arguing voices. As a result we walk around with double messages constantly firing off in our minds. The effect not only makes us feel schizophrenic, but it erodes our sense of self worth because the negative voice often shouts down the positive one. Self-esteem – the art of feeling lovable – becomes a catch twenty-two. We feel lovable when we know others love us but unless we feel as if we're lovable, we resist love. The only way to accept love from another is to first hear a clear, consistent message that makes us believe that we are lovable.

After receiving The Message I discovered how deceptively simple it is. As I began to absorb its lessons, I realized that it demanded nothing less than a 180-degree shift in my perception. Seeing the outside world from a totally different point of view was a prerequisite to being able to see myself differently. This was the essence as well as the goal the message had given me. Eventually, after years of practice, I began to notice that the negative voice (and sometimes there are more than one) began to give way to the positive, ceaseless, repetitive waves of "You are beautiful." A real and palpable sense of peace began to wash over me. My mind was then able to clear itself long enough to let an occasional strong and encouraging thought get through.

It takes practice and a lot of self-discipline to keep one clear and consistent voice in my head. I can tell I've made progress because I don't feel as vulnerable as I used to feel. All my various and disconnected parts seem to have become integrated. I see myself differently. As a result I relate to everyone else differently. I used to hide behind my wall. Now that I feel connected, I don't need that wall. Maybe it's as simple as this: when you feel you're lovable, you are free to act lovingly, even toward yourself.

LAST THOUGHTS

Here are eight points to help you keep your focus along the way:

- ❖ Your best teachers offer you your most difficult lessons. Often they are also the same people you "love to hate."

- ❖ Your wall is your line of defense, but to others it looks like a line of attack.

- ❖ Look at your grudges. They all come from the past. Choose to keep your grudges or forget them but stop pretending you don't have any.

- ❖ Be congruent. Match what you do and what you say.

- ❖ Balance your thoughts and emotions.

- ❖ Be aware that every interaction with another gives you an opportunity to be yourself. Practice and be patient.

- ❖ The purpose of your life on earth is to wake up. Your relationships provide you with the lessons you need to learn.

- ❖ Be grateful.

After many years of reflection and change, I have wondered if it was Eric himself who sent me the message "You are beautiful," this time from Heaven. Did he realize that I had not understood it the first time while he was on Earth? Certainly he would have remembered how much self-doubt I felt; how before I could love myself, I would need permission from someone I knew and trusted. He also would have known that I would pass on to others his gift to me through my work.

I hope the following lessons will resonate with your heart and mind. I hope you will give yourself the opportunity to practice each step along the way. If you are not ready to receive the words, at least give yourself permission to consider that seeing yourself as "beautiful" is possible. You can learn, as I have, that you are lovable because love is all there is. You need no other reason.

Imagine what it would have been like if,
from the moment you were conceived,
in this body,
you had been told how beautiful you really are.

Imagine what it would be like
to have people acknowledge you as beautiful.
And then you will understand
the gift you are giving yourself.

THE MESSAGE

A Message of Love

1

THE WALL

1 – the wall

When you were a little child
You began to build a wall
And now that wall is so thick and so high
You are afraid to tear it down.
Life is familiar behind the wall.
Anything is better than tearing it down.
Anything.
Even pain and illness.
Even relationships that go nowhere.
Even life without joy.
Even death.

Close your eyes and imagine your wall.

Describe your wall.
How tall, how wide, how thick is it?
What is it made of?
Touch it. How does it feel?

Draw a picture of your wall.

You built it as a child in order to survive.
You built it because you thought you needed it
To protect you against people who reject you,
Who leave you,
Who don't love you.
You built it because you thought
If you separated yourself from others
They could not hurt you.

Has your wall protected you?

How?

How has it not protected you?

Now, take a moment to step back and look at that wall.
Admire it.
How hard you worked to build it.
Consider what you have put into it.
Every part was laid with pain and resistance.
Your pain,
Your resistance.
You have defended yourself so well you think
The wall is invisible...
To everyone.

It is not invisible.
We see it every time you smile and your eyes are sad.
We see it every time you say one thing and mean another.
We see it when you want to speak what you really feel
But don't because you think
The other person will laugh at you,
Or reject you,
Or ignore you.

We see it every time you swallow all those words.
Every time you deny who you are
And what you truly want
We see how thick,
How wide,
How high that wall is.

But you pretend that it's invisible
And all the people out there pretend,
Just as you do,
That the wall is not there.
You pretend and they pretend.

You can deny that you built your own wall.
You can say others built it for you
And you can blame them.
That you built it to survive is true...
When you were small.
Now that you are an adult people are your size.
Everyone is your peer.
A child is vulnerable,
An adult does not need to be.
There is no one to blame.
Not even yourself.

*Practice noticing your wall. Watch how it appears
every time you want to pull away from others.*

*See how it appears every time you avoid, you deny,
or you pretend.
See it appear when you're angry and blaming.*

*Notice how you feel when you push others away.
Notice how you feel when you let them push you away.*

Look back.
Look at the faces, the scenes from the past.
The hurt. The blame. The anger.
What you are seeing are the defenses,
The artful games of pretense and sabotage,
Yours
And theirs.

What has happened is already in the past
And the past cannot be changed.
It doesn't exist.
Only the memory of it exists.
As a child you felt afraid,
Your fear now is simply a memory of that old fear.
It lived with you behind your wall
And you built your wall in order to contain that fear.
It is pointless to go back and fix what is no more.
There is nothing to fix.

The wall has served its purpose.
It was built by you because you thought you needed it
In order to survive.
You have survived.
It has done its job.

So the question is, do you still need to live behind it?
Or can you now, in search of Self,
In search of You,
Can you now begin
To take the pieces down?

You will resist change.

As you open your mind to the possibility that
you are a spiritual being – not merely a physical
being – you will resist change. You will even
resist positive transformational change. The image
you see in the mirror everyday is an illusion, a
reflection of how you see yourself and how others
see you. It is not who you are.

You have been projecting this illusion to the
world and to yourself for a long time. You've
become used to living behind a wall. You believe
that unless you continue to hide yourself you
will appear naked and vulnerable to the world.
This is why you will resist change. You are afraid.

2

THE REASON WE'RE HERE

The reason we're here is because we are evolving.
The body is born in a tight, painful space.
It lives,
It feels pain, fear, grief, love, joy, ecstasy, frustration,
Symptoms,
And the body dies.
But the soul, your soul
Goes to another place in the universal consciousness
And then, when it is time,
Chooses another body and comes back again.
The soul does not die.

You have similar relationships with the same souls
In different bodies
From lifetime to lifetime.
As the faces change and the events change,
The relationship evolves.
Often, it is the same conflict
But in different relationships.

You have chosen patterns and themes in order to learn
The lesson of love.
That is the evolution of the soul.
But you allow your conflict and pain and symptoms
To hold you back because you are afraid of change.

You resist change.
That is all right.
We all resist change.
Yet change is the one thing that makes the difference
Because it is the effect of a cause.
Once change is manifested,
First in you,
Then in the loved ones you see daily
Or think of daily,
It moves to the outer world,
To the market, to the street, to your government,
To people in other worlds on this planet
And beyond.

The beauty within you, once you see it,
Will manifest change in you
Which then manifests change in your loved ones
Which manifests change in the world.

When you resist seeing yourself as a beautiful being,
You resist loving yourself.
Your conscious programming has dulled
The awareness of the truth which is that
You are,
You have been,
You will be.

You are indestructible.
The coping mechanisms, the symptoms, the defenses,
The pain, the conflicts,
All of these were built into the wall
Which you decided to construct
When you were small
In order to adapt yourself to your family.
You have allowed your conscious mind to be programmed
From the time you were conceived.

Take 3 long, slow, deep breaths.
Imagine yourself floating above the earth plane.
Take your time.

See your body below you. Experience being light ...
light ... lighter ... until you have no weight at all.

Notice how you feel.

You are experiencing conflict.

When you watch a baby learning how to stand, observe how many times the baby reaches out to grab a stable support system – such as the leg of a table – and observe how many times the baby falls down. His body is awkward, unsure. But look at his face. He is determined. He is focused. He barely cries when he falls down because he is so eager to get up again. He is not discouraged when he falls. He simply keeps practicing until one day he stands up and stays up. All by himself. And when he succeeds look at his face again. Notice the joy.

The baby has no inner voice that tells him he "shouldn't" or that he "can't." In fact he has no sense of conflict about what he his doing. He is responding to inside information that tells him this is what he must do next. You, like the baby, have a challenge before you, something you must do next. But, unlike the baby, you are experiencing conflict.

3

MISUNDERSTANDINGS
AND ILLUSIONS

When you were in your mother's womb, you felt her.
You heard her voice.
You felt your father. You heard his voice.
All the waves came through neurologically
From their systems to yours.
Their outer world affected you within that microcosm,
The uterus, the birth sac,
The place where you grew and evolved first in this body,
Until you were physically able to be born.
Until you were physically able to cope
With the tasks of life.

As a member of your family you had to learn
What it was that you thought you needed to do
In order to survive.

All families are the same, yet different.
Who says what, what the rules are,
All those things you learned early in order to cope,
In order to survive,
And you learned those rules, as every child learns,
Through your senses.
You absorbed what was unconsciously as well as consciously
Expected of you
And the rules that were not spoken
You learned better than the rules
That were spoken.

All those rules,
Both the implicit and the explicit rules,
Were planted firmly into your being
And these are the rules
By which you function today.

What did your parents do when there was conflict?
What do you do when there is conflict?

Is it the same?

Is it the opposite?

Your conscious mind may be in touch
With a great many of the rules.
But there are other rules which your unconscious mind
Has not brought to light
Which deeply affect the way you behave.
If, for example, you say,
"I am not lovable. I am not eternal,"
Then you know that your conscious mind
Has denied the very essence of your being.

You have let your conscious mind be programmed to do that.
If you wipe away those thoughts
And look into your unconscious,
You will begin to see a perfect soul within
And you will begin to love yourself.

What remains is a matter of changing the conscious programming
That you thought you had to learn as a child,
In this life, in this body, with this family.

You have come into this life with memory, soul memory
From other lifetimes and other relationships,
But you are in this lifetime in order to change,
In order to evolve,
In order to look at what really is.
Not at what you have allowed your conscious mind
To seduce you into believing.

The voices of your parents
Have led you to believe certain things.
But what parents do best is teach their expectations of you
Rather than teach you to be open
To your own dreams and expectations.
That is why you chose them as your parents,
In order to learn what you came to learn.
So there is a misunderstanding
That starts from the moment of conception.

Looking upon them as parents is where
The misunderstanding begins.
It seems as if what they have taught you best
Is how they want you to be,
Instead of helping you find your own way.

But, if you look upon them as teachers,
Carefully chosen to teach you
The perfect lesson for you to learn,
You will understand that they are here
To help you realize who you are.
No one can do this lesson for you,
Yet this lesson must be learned.

As you find your way, be aware that you are not alone.
You are part of the universal consciousness.
You are eternal.
You are love itself.
But you do not believe that
And you do not act in that belief.

What have your parents expected of you?
What have you expected of them?

How have they let you down?
How have you let them down?

See yourself attached to them with a long cord.
How does it feel?
Notice your body.

Give others time to adapt to you.

As the baby practices standing up, there are adoring faces surrounding him; smiling, encouraging
faces urging him on. But some of the people
surrounding you may not encourage you in your
practice. Some may even escalate their old behav-
ior. They have become as stiff and rigid in their
patterns as you have in yours. You've been wear-
ing your mask a long time. They don't recognize
you without it. Where have you gone? Give others
time to adapt to you.

Change always seems threatening, yet change is
like skipping a smooth stone across the water and
watching the ripples every time the stone touches
down. The ripples simply indicate that the stone
has touched the water's surface. Nothing more.

4

STARTING OVER

Let the idea grow in you that you can start over.
Begin to realize that the past was the way it was
Because you did not know you are
A beautiful, eternal being.
Say to yourself, "I am moving on. I am starting over.
Even with some of the same faces.
Because this moment is the only time that exists,
I can only change what is now in this moment."

You will begin to notice
That your wall is not as important as it once was.
You do appreciate it.
You have treated it with care.
With your wall up you moved the same parts of you
Over and over again.
As your wall begins to come down
You will begin to move different parts of you.
More of you.

Move all the various parts of you...

Your shoulders, your face, your toes...

Feel energy flowing into parts that are stiff and unused.

If you use your head a great deal
To analyze,
To think,
To struggle for answers,
Move into your body away from your head
Because you have taught yourself to use your head
Instead of feeling.

When people speak to you, feel the words.
When people look at you and touch you,
Feel the way the look and the touch really are.
Allow yourself to take time to feel.
And when your head begins to think, to judge, to analyze,
Pause.
Breathe deeply.

Stay with the moment
Because this is the moment change takes place.
You will find that feeling will become easier.
Even though you think you are afraid,
The fear is totally irrelevant.
The feeling of being afraid now
Is a memory of an old fear.
The fear itself does not exist in the present.

Allow yourself to wallow.

To suffer.

To feel sorry for yourself.

Let all your feelings rise to the surface.

Let them be.

If you are a person who is very much in your body,
If you are a person who feels and interprets
Through feeling,
You often feel overwhelmed.
You feel powerless. Helpless.
That is only because you have not, in the past,
Used your reason.
Allow yourself now, when the feelings come,
To let your head lead you.
Think clearly.
Focus clearly.

Let your reason guide you.
Think before you speak.
Say what you mean.

All the parts of the body must be in balance.
When your thoughts and your feelings are in conflict,
There is no peace inside you
Therefore, there is no peace outside, in the world.
When you are off balance, you need the wall to protect you.
When you are in balance, you do not.

If in the past you responded with emotions,
Practice using your head.

If in the past, you responded with your head,
Practice feeling.

Practice, practice, practice. Habits die hard!

You will probably feel as if you're losing yourself.

As you begin to see yourself and others differently, you will probably feel as if you're losing yourself. As if you're losing control. That's why you've
been afraid to change. Yes, but with practice you
will discover the image you've been projecting all
your life is not who you are. You will realize it
has been an illusion all along.

5

MOVING ON

So, what are we about?
What is the point to all this?
It certainly doesn't seem to be the point to live vainly,
To look in the mirror and see the reflection
Of that face and that body,
For that face and that body will change and age
And eventually go away,
Never to be seen again.
Except in memory.

Something is missing from that image in the mirror.
What *is* missing?
Seeing you as you are.
A beautiful, loving being.

When you look into the mirror, look at your eyes.
Look at your mouth.
Does the mouth smile when the eyes are sad?
Do you hope to fool yourself as you look in the mirror
And then fool your loved ones and your friends
And the people you work with?
Do you count on the fact that we just look at the smile
And avoid the eyes in order not to see?

Behind the face is another place to hide.
When you look in the mirror and see your face
And not the soul within,
You are looking at the barriers,
The coping mechanisms,
The inventiveness that you have created
From the time you were born.

Coping gets you from today to tomorrow,
But coping isn't living.
Coping is surviving.

Look inside
Beyond the face to your own soul.
When you see the soul within you,
You will see the soul within everyone.
It is there you will find perfect love
For we are all the same.

Look in the mirror. See your face as a mask.
What thoughts and feelings does the mask hide?

Take off the mask.
What do you see?

Take your time.
You have eternity.
You are here now.
You will be here again.
We cannot measure time in seconds, minutes and hours.
We think we can,
But when you know your soul is eternal
You know time is abundant.

So, you may begin change now,
You may go slowly.
You may begin later.
You may go quickly.
It is completely up to you.
When you love yourself, you will make time for love.

You are a beautiful, eternal soul
In this body
In this lifetime
To evolve
And
To change.

Close your eyes and breathe 3 long, slow, deep breaths.
Inhaling, focus on the word "peace,"
Exhaling, focus on the words "letting go."

Feel the chair under you.
Listen to the sounds in the room, in the street.
Be still for 15 minutes.

Practice.

> You believe that if you give up
> your need to "control," you will
> become powerless.

To grow, to evolve, you can no longer base your
reality on what you think you see – your own
projection of the world reflected back. You
believe that you are vulnerable. You believe that
you need to live behind a wall. You believe that
if you give up your need to "control," you will
become powerless. This is a mistake. In fact,
the opposite is true.

Both people and events exist outside of you,
beyond your control, where no real power exists.
This single truth will empower you in a way you
never dreamed possible. It will set you free. Alter
your perception of the world – change how you
see – and you will understand.

6

AWAKENING

Imagine what it would have been like
If from the moment you were conceived in this body
You had been told, "You are beautiful."

Imagine what it would be like to have people acknowledge you
As a beautiful, lovable being.

If you believed that you were lovable
You would begin to act loving.
People would notice you.
People would smile.
People would want to be with you.
They would know that if they stayed with you for any time
They would feel loved.
This would give them hope.
They would know, if you could love them,
They could love themselves.

Imagine that.

See yourself as a teacher with everyone you meet.
Are you teaching lessons of love or lessons of fear?
(You can tell by the way people respond to you.)

Notice how you feel when people want to be with you.
Notice how you feel when they put up their walls.

Once you begin to accept yourself as lovable,
You will love you.
You will begin to think kindly of you.
You will begin to be kind to you.
You will notice how boundless love is.
All your relationships will begin to change.
You will be aware that everyone is a reflection of you.

Everyone has a wall just like you.
Like you everyone is living in fear of being hurt.

You will be aware
That the only difference between you and them
Is how high
How thick
How strong their wall is.

As you begin to see you in them
And as you begin to see them in you,
You will not need to protect yourself
Or defend yourself
Because you will know when other people are being kind
Or not.
And you will know when other people are being helpful
Or not.
You will know because they do as you do.
And you see in them exactly what is in you.
So you need never fear that you will be hurt in any way.
You will be, simply, more aware.

Love is not static.
It is evolving, yet never changing.
Awareness of love
Increases.
As you see beauty within you,
And as you know that you are lovable,
The awareness of love,
First for you and then, as a matter of course,
For everyone else,
Will change the way you see yourself
And the way you appreciate yourself.
Once that is changed,
You will behave in a different manner
With everyone around you.
Then they will begin to see with different eyes.

Love and change go together.

When you feel a grudge coming on, try a new thought.
You can choose to feel LOVE (joy, happiness, peace)
or FEAR (anger, resentment, blame).

Notice that you must make a choice.
Notice you cannot feel loving and be afraid at the same time.

Try it.

First comes that awareness, that awakening.
Then there is something you do differently.
A relationship begins to change.
The body feels more energy,
More joy.
There is a lightness and a humor.
Perhaps life isn't as serious as you once thought it was.
All the harsh memories begin to soften.

You will feel awkward in the beginning.
You can expect that.
Once you have become aware,
Once there is that deep stirring within you,
Once there is that beginning,
That hungering to know who you are,
Change has already begun
Because you no longer accept things the way they have been.

As you begin to accept yourself as lovable,
Which you always have been,
Which you are
And which you will always be,
Let yourself think it every moment you remember.

See the face of someone who has upset you.
See him as afraid. Notice his wall.
See how he hides behind it by attacking you
because he is defending himself.

If you changed places, would the picture be the same?

Never give up.

As your perception shifts, you will experience new
joy and excitement one moment and old fear and
confusion the next. This is normal and natural.
You are waking up. Awakening to the idea that
you are lovable, that you are beautiful and that
you are spirit, comes with a new consciousness
that is realized only through radical change in
the way you think, the way you see, and the way
you behave.

Never give up. Like the baby stay focused.
Practice. When you fall down, get up. Reach
out for the table leg whenever you need support.
The adoring faces surrounding you and encourag-
ing you may not be the ones that you expect.
They are there because they believe in you.
They *want* you to succeed.

7

ACCEPT THE BEAUTY WITHIN

Imagine what it would have been like
If from the moment you were conceived,
In this body,
You had been told how beautiful you really are.
Imagine what it would be like to have people acknowledge you
As beautiful.
And then you will understand the gift you are giving yourself.

You are a beautiful, eternal soul
Who is in this body in this lifetime
To evolve
And
To change.

You were taught incorrectly, not out of malice,
but out of ignorance.

To correct your own vision, practice seeing yourself
and all others as beautiful. Lovable.
Practice with everyone you meet.

This is the way to correct the original mistake.

You must love yourself first.

There is no change without risk. As you begin to see yourself as lovable and deserving of kindness, disrespect in all its forms will be inconsistent with your new awareness. Those who do not see you as an equal may not change. They may reject you. They do not see themselves as lovable so they are afraid of love. The truth is simple: only when we love ourselves can we love others.

Seeking love from others so you can feel lovable does not work. You must love yourself first. Then you will effect change in others. Love yourself, keep your mind and heart clear, and your love and compassion for others will be evident. We are never healed alone. Every change touches someone else and affects someone else. Love is catching. You will see.

One day you will no longer be the baby learning to stand. One day you will be able to stand alone. When you do, look at your face in the mirror. Notice the joy.

If you are beautiful when
you are born
you can thank your parents.

If you are beautiful when
you die
you can thank yourself.

– old Japanese axiom my mother used to tell me

IT TAKES A VILLAGE

I don't think anyone is prepared for a mystic experience. It comes with no warning, lifts you up body and soul and leaves you in a place you've never been. With a radical new awareness. It's as if a great secret has been revealed to you and you've been singled out to pass it on. The experience puts you completely outside yourself, evoking a sensation of separateness. Aloneness. It wasn't until people started showing up to help me that I began to understand that I was neither separate nor alone.

Furthermore, I understood I would never feel alone again. Even now, as I go through the names of those who began to appear in my life, it's amazing to realize how many there were, almost immediately. And how many there still are. And how many more there are going to be. Obviously, once given, this new awareness was never intended for me to take on alone.

My husband, Valerio was the first on the scene. He came through the garden gate around 5:00 o'clock just as Side A of the tape had ended and clicked off. I said something like, "I don't know what just happened but here, will you listen with me?" Valerio nodded and lit a cigarette. I pressed the rewind button and then play, and for the first time we both heard "The Message." As the sound of my voice came through the recorder, he stood transfixed by the kitchen door for the full 28 minutes, listening. We didn't say much afterward but I remember feeling relieved. I now had someone else who had shared the experience and trusted it as I did.

Elaine Giamona, my assistant, entered the circle next. Her previous job had been with Virginia Satir, a pioneer in the family therapy movement at M.R.I. in Palo Alto. Satir, well-known as an author and lecturer, felt strongly about the spiritual component in the art of healing. That's why, when I asked Elaine to transcribe The Message – which by now filled two sides of a 60 minute tape – on the computer, I felt confident she wouldn't think I was crazy. On the contrary, from the very beginning Elaine expressed her eagerness to help me find a way to bring The Message to others.

Sarah Bernstein, a born marketing genius, single-handedly helped the original tape succeed. She was in charge of the new "Whole Life Center" at The Thunderbird Bookstore in Carmel. The center brought in hundreds of customers who were being swept along in the new wave of consciousness by everything spiritual. She pushed *You Are Beautiful* to anyone who came through the doors and invited me to speak at public gatherings there. As a result, the network of people who heard The Message and told others to buy the tape widened considerably.

Eldon Dedini, an old friend and a brilliant cartoonist came next. I called him when I began to think about making *You Are Beautiful* into a book. A man of enormous generosity and kindness to friends and the community, he enthusiastically agreed to help. I also called April Streeter, who had bought one of the first Macs and was experimenting with desktop publishing. She edited and organized The Message around Eldon's first drawings. This was in the mid-eighties. But at a certain point I let the project drop until several years ago when Eldon and I took another look at what we had. Eldon added some new illustrations and helped the little character, which plays the child in the story, evolve into an adorable androgynous humanoid. Based on what

April and I had originally done together almost twenty years before, I finished the manuscript. Bunne Hartmann, a graphic designer I've worked with a long time, took over from there. Bunne also did my first book, *The New Family: Mapping Your Way To The Good Stuff!* which was published online in 2000.

Rick Chelew, of Oral Traditions, is a gifted musician and sound engineer. We have collaborated on many projects and produced audio tapes of my talks and retreats. He has brought the CD into its new incarnation and remains a solid member of the team. A special thanks also to Robert Idriartborde who – long before digital technology – spent many hours with me in the sound studio engineering the original mix. The three musicians who bring the elegant music of Saint-Saëns, Satie, Debussy, Harrison, Brahms, Rabaud, and Beauchamp to the "you are beautiful" experience are Sue Ammond on clarinet, Pauline Thomas Troia on piano and Beverly Bellows on the harp.

Track One of the CD invites you to spend a few moments of relaxation before The Message begins. It also brings into this project my spiritual teacher, the Russian born Indra Devi. I still remember her magic. She would fly through the rooms of her Hatha Yoga school in Tecate, Baja California in her orange sari – arms outstretched in greeting to all her students. Mataji – little mother as she liked us to call her – was already in her eighties when we met in 1974. Petite and unconditionally feminine she would laugh with joy when I teased her that she was secretly a social butterfly posing as a Yogi. Her book, *Yoga For Americans* which was published in 1959, was written for the layman. It was the first of its kind and became an instant classic. I have used the words of her meditation to guide you through *Savasana* – The Relaxation Pose. Her presence blesses us all.

My friend and editor Elliot Ruchowitz Roberts took on the ultimate challenge of editing The Message without altering its original rhythm, content and feel. Also many thanks to my friends Alan Jardine, Dick Dalsemer, Biff Smith, Carole Erickson, Mort Levitt, Deborah Jacroux, Lisa Vandersluis, Carrol Barrie, Caroline Pincus, Robin Sawyer, Marilyn Anton, Amy and Peter Figge, Joan Little, Louise Coffey-Webb, Cece and Larry Chazen, Giulio Dedini, my husband Valerio and our family Diana and Steve Houx, and Livia and Scott James for looking at the book and giving me feedback on the CD.

Amy Essick, Art Curator for Monterey Community Hospital deserves a special medal. She envisioned *You Are Beautiful* as a book from the beginning. A woman of great taste and knowledge, she has never wavered in her belief in the project.

My gratitude to the many have who have been kind enough to endorse *You Are Beautiful* and whose prayers for success go with the book. I thank you. And to all of my clients over the years, you have been my teachers and continue to be part of my extended family. Thank you for your love, your courage to change and your trust.

And then of course, there are my angels. I've been aware of them for some time now and I'm quite sure there are three. I often feel them whisper by – guiding me, protecting me and giving me pep talks. They seem to be around most when I'm in the shower or driving. Don't ask me why. Every village needs angels.

© 2005 Valerio Giusi

NADYA GIUSI

Nadya Giusi has worked with families for forty-five years. Before becoming a marriage and family therapist in 1980, Giusi pioneered Montessori education on the Monterey Peninsula, establishing three schools and a teacher training center. In 2003 Giusi founded FAMILIES FOR ATTITUDI-NAL HEALING, a non-judgmental educational approach dedicated to fostering peace-centered relationships in the family and in the world. A member of the adjunct faculty at Monterey Peninsula College, Giusi also maintains a private practice, offers classes and workshops in the community and is an author. *You Are Beautiful* is Giusi's second book. She and her husband, Valerio, have been married 50 years, have two daughters and five grandchildren and live in Carmel-by-the-Sea, California.

ELDON DEDINI

Award-winning cartoonist Eldon Dedini's career has spanned
more than five decades. A native of King City, California,
Dedini graduated from Chouinard Art Institute in Los Angeles.
He began his professional career as a cartoonist for the *Salinas
Morning Post* before moving on to work at Walt Disney
Studios. From 1946 to 1950, he was a member of the staff
at *Esquire* magazine. Dedini then went to work for *The New
Yorker*, where he has been a contract cartoonist for many
years. He is currently also a contract cartoonist for *Playboy*.
On four occasions Dedini has been honored with the Best
Magazine Cartoonist Award from the National Cartoonists
Society. Widely published, Dedini's work has also appeared
in *Punch* and *Sports Illustrated*. Eldon Dedini resides in
Carmel, California, with his wife, Virginia.

NOTES